How We Get Food

by Erin Duffy

 HOUGHTON MIFFLIN BOSTON

PHOTOGRAPHY CREDITS: Cover © Rosenfeld/Corbis; 1 © Corbis: 2 © Rosenfeld/Corbis; 3 Nick Daly/Getty Images/Photonica; 4 © Michael Boys/Corbis; 5 © PhotoDisc; 6 © Kevin Fleming/Corbis; 7 © Jim West/Alamy; 8 © Jim West/Alamy; 9 © Somos Images/Corbis; 10 © Corbis

Printed in China

ISBN-13: 978-0-547-02989-4
ISBN-10: 0-547-02989-6

2 3 4 5 6 7 8 9 0940 15 14 13 12 11 10

food

Look at all the food!
The food is on the table.
How do I get my food?
How do you get your food?

ground

garden

Some people have a garden
at home. They grow fruits and
vegetables. First, they plant
seeds under the ground.
Then they water the seeds.
Seeds need water and sunlight
to grow bigger.

vegetables

The plants grow bigger.
Soon we will have fruits
and vegetables.
The fruits and vegetables start
in the garden.
Then the fruits and vegetables
can go right on your table.

farm

Some farmers have a small farm.
They grow food.
Some farmers have fields.
They grow wheat or vegetables.
Some farmers have animals.
They have chickens and cows.
Some farmers have fruit trees.

farmer

Farmers work a lot.
Farmers water the plants we
need for food.
Then the plants grow bigger.
Farmers feed the animals.
Then the animals grow bigger.

market

Farmers get food from the fields
and farms. Farmers get the
milk from the cows.
Farmers get the eggs
from the chickens.
Farmers sell these foods at
a market.
People buy these foods.

Farms can be big or small.
Big farms have lots of plants
for food, and lots of animals.
Lots of people work on big
farms. These people get the
plants we need. These people
feed the animals, too.

Sometimes trucks or trains
can take the food to cities.
Trucks or trains can take the
food to towns, too.
Then you can buy the food
at a store.

We can get food
from many places.
We can get food from a
garden or from a farm.
We can buy food
at a market or at a store.
How do people get food?
How do you get your food?

Responding

Author's Purpose

Why did the author write this story? What three details in the story tell you this? Make a chart.

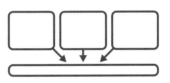

✏ **Talk About It**

Text to World Think of a fruit or vegetable to eat. Where is it from?

✔ **TARGET SKILL** **Author's Purpose**

Tell why an author writes a book.

✔ **TARGET STRATEGY** **Summarize**

Stop to tell important ideas as you read.

GENRE Informational text gives facts about a topic.